Contents

Words shown in **bold** in the text are explained in the glossary.

All the places in this book are shown on the map on page 22.

It's Time to Play!

In Thailand, skipping is a popular game. Children make their own long ropes by looping lots of rubber bands together.

In the United States, a broom handle and a tennis ball are all that's needed for a game of stickball.

In France, boys and girls hold on tight to this roundabout.

These boys in Ethiopia are enjoying an outdoor game of table football.

Wheelbarrow rides are great fun for these children in Vietnam.

A Game of Football

A game of football in Brazil

All around the world, children love to play football.

Many children live in **poverty**, though.

Their families cannot afford to buy them footballs.

So young players make their own footballs from plastic bags!

These boys in Kenya are making a football.

One way to make a football is to pack scrunched-up newspaper inside a plastic bag. Then the first bag is covered with up to 30 more bags. Finally, the ball of bags is held together with rubber bands or string.

Time for kick-off!

Riding a Bike

Riding a bike is a popular pastime for children all over the world.

In many parts of Africa, kids and adults ride bikes made of wood.

Wooden bikes are used for more than just having fun. They are also used to carry goods such as fruit, vegetables and firewood.

Rolling Tyres

An old tyre might look like a piece of junk but it can easily become a new toy.

In many parts of the world, children look for old tyres on rubbish dumps.

Then they have fun rolling and chasing their tyres.

It takes skill to keep a tyre rolling or make it change direction. These boys in India are using sticks to control their tyres.

Kids compete to see who can roll their tyre the fastest and furthest.

It's Fun to Swing

Up and down. Up and down. All over the world,
kids love to play on swings.

You can swing on an old tyre.

You can swing in a playground.

These Baka children live in a **rainforest** in Cameroon.

They have made a swing out of liana vines.

A liana vine

Liana vines are plants with long, thin, bendy stems. The vines grow up from the ground and get tangled in tree branches. Then the vines dangle back down like ropes.

13

Let's Play Tug-of-War

In Vietnam, tug-of-war has been a **traditional** contest for centuries.

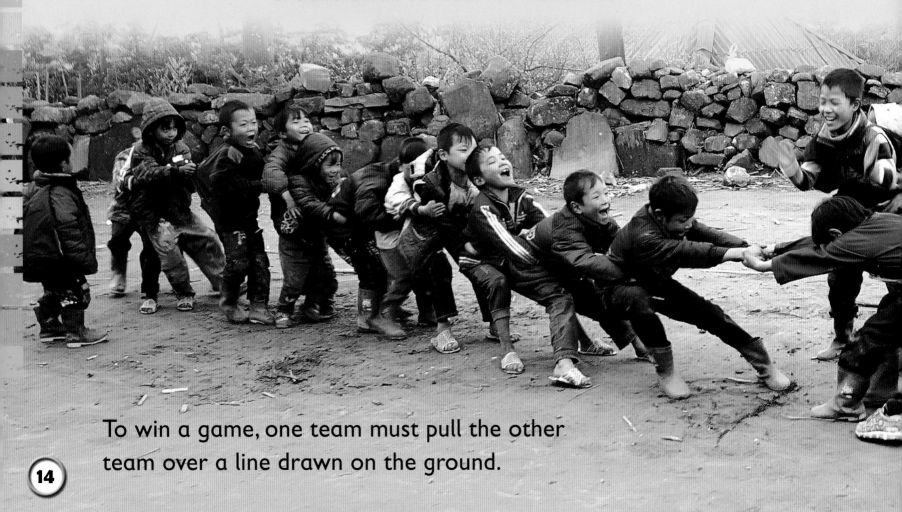

To win a game, one team must pull the other team over a line drawn on the ground.

Tug-of-war teams usually pull on a rope.

Sometimes, however, children just hold onto each other and pull hard!

Kite Fighting and Running

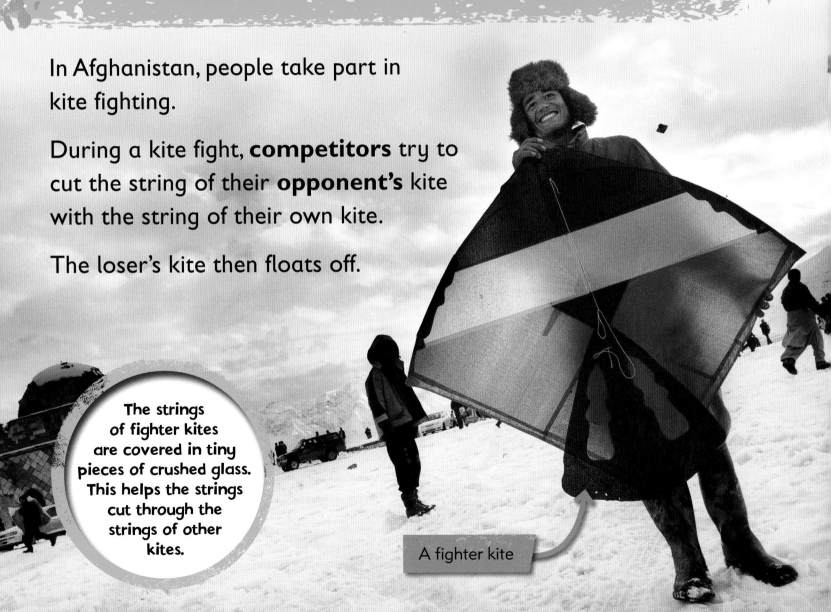

In Afghanistan, people take part in kite fighting.

During a kite fight, **competitors** try to cut the string of their **opponent's** kite with the string of their own kite.

The loser's kite then floats off.

The strings of fighter kites are covered in tiny pieces of crushed glass. This helps the strings cut through the strings of other kites.

A fighter kite

Children and grown-ups
chase after kites that have
been cut free.

This is called kite running.

The kite runner who catches
a free kite gets to keep it!

These boys are chasing
after a small kite.

Winning Rubber Bands

In many parts of South-east Asia, children like to play a game with rubber bands.

Each player places a rubber band on the ground.

Then the players begin blowing on their rubber bands.

The object of the game is to blow your rubber band on top of your opponent's.

The winner of a game keeps both rubber bands. Young players learn their skills by watching older kids and getting lots of practise.

Our Favourite Toys

All over the world, children love to play with their favourite toys.

These boys are sailing their homemade boats in the sea.

This toy bus is made out of wire and other pieces of rubbish.

This girl loves her doll made from the leaves of a banana plant.

It's a challenge to balance and run on coconut shells.

Where in the World?

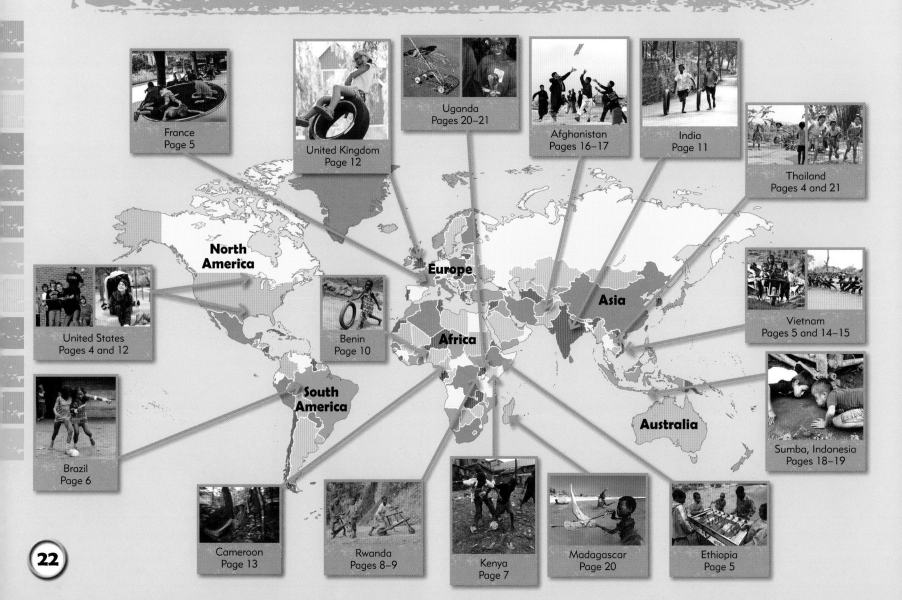

France
Page 5

United Kingdom
Page 12

Uganda
Pages 20–21

Afghanistan
Pages 16–17

India
Page 11

Thailand
Pages 4 and 21

North
America

Europe

Asia

United States
Pages 4 and 12

Benin
Page 10

Africa

Vietnam
Pages 5 and 14–15

South
America

Australia

Sumba, Indonesia
Pages 18–19

Brazil
Page 6

Cameroon
Page 13

Rwanda
Pages 8–9

Kenya
Page 7

Madagascar
Page 20

Ethiopia
Page 5

Glossary

competitor
A person who takes part, or competes, in a game or sport.

opponent
The person playing against you in a game or sport.

poverty
Being very poor without enough money to buy essential things such as food or fuel.

rainforest
A thick forest of tall trees and other plants where lots of rain falls.

traditional
Something that has been done in a certain way for many years by a group of people. For example, playing a game or taking part in a sport.

Index

Learn More Online

To learn more about play
around the world, go to
www.rubytuesdaybooks.com/play